MUSIC TO HONOUR
GOD'S NAME

MUSIC TO HONOUR GOD'S NAME

Accompaniment for Liturgical Music from *Alive-O* and *Beo go Deo*

Compiled by
Patricia Hegarty and Mary Nugent

VERITAS

First published 2000 by
Veritas Publications
7/8 Lower Abbey Street
Dublin 1

ISBN 1 85390 555 0

Cover design by Bill Bolger
Illustrations by Jeanette Dunne
Music setting by Playright Music Ltd, Dublin
Typesetting by Colette Dower, Veritas Publications
Printed in the Republic of Ireland by Paceprint Ltd, Dublin

Contents

Liturgical Index

Preface

The hymns and songs that we all learnt as children are perhaps those that will stay with us throughout our lives and will have special significance for us. This new volume of accompaniments is a welcome resource for providing 'child-friendly' liturgical music that will have a lasting influence on our children. It will be useful not only in the school context, but also at the increasing number of family Masses being celebrated in parishes on Sundays.

Of particular importance, from a liturgical point of view, are the acclamations from the two Mass settings. Singing these parts of the Mass will help to bring them alive for the children and will help to insert them deeper into the key moments of the liturgy. These settings can supplement the *Mass of Peace* by Seoirse Bodley, which is already well known and easily accessible. The provision of two simple psalm settings is also an important feature, and it would be wonderful if our children could experience the singing of the Responsorial Psalm as the norm rather than the exception.

The material in this book is mostly new, although a few old favourites are included. Some very well-known pieces have accompaniments which are easily found elsewhere, and so have not been included in this volume. There is a good mix of material in both Irish and English. It is hoped that, whatever the principal language of the children, they would be helped to sing in both languages. Irish translations of texts are not intended as exact renderings of the original meaning; rather they seek to convey in a new way the overall sense of the original. Some of the pieces will work for a variety of different contexts, other than those mentioned in the index of categories. Teachers should also feel free to choose from any pieces those verses they believe to be most suitable.

John McCann

Alleluia

Bernard Sexton

Al - le - lu - ia, al - le - lu - ia, al - le - lu - ia.

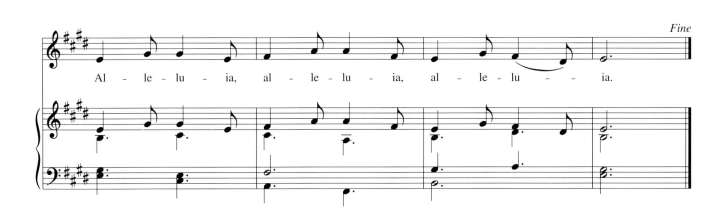

Fine

Al - le - lu - ia, al - le - lu - ia, al - le - lu - ia.

Je - sus is ris - en. He has saved his peo - ple.

D'ais - éir - igh Ío - sa. Shábh - áil sé 'n cin - ne daon - na.

[S.W.]

D. C. al Fine

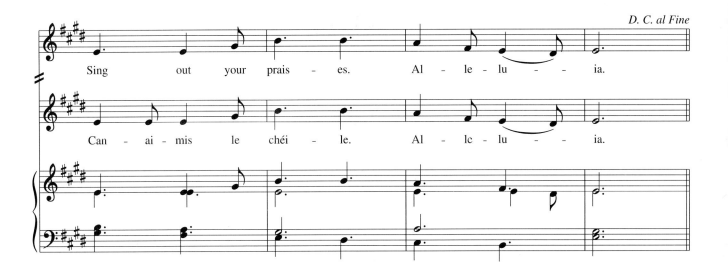

Sing out your prais - es. Al - le - lu - - ia.

Can - ai - mis le chéi - le. Al - lc - lu - - ia.

Blessed Be God

John McCann

Bles - sed be God! Bles - sed be God! Bles - sed be God __ for e - ver!

1. Let us pre - pare the ta - ble, the ta - ble of __ the Lord, _____ with

cloths __ so white, so gleam - ing bright, Bles - sed be God for e - ver!

2. Let us prepare the table, the table of the Lord,
   With shining light of candles bright.
   Blessed be God forever!

3. Let us bring bread together to the table of the Lord.
   It will become the bread of life.
   Blessed be God forever!

4. Let us bring wine together to the table of the Lord.
   It will become the blood of Christ.
   Blessed be God forever!

5. Let us give thanks to God who loves and feeds all people,
   Let us give praise, let us give thanks.
   Blessed be God forever!

Note: *Verses 1 and 2 may be omitted if the altar is not being dressed at the Preparation of Gifts.*

Céad Míle Fáilte Romhat

Traidisiúnta

2. Glóir agus moladh duit, a Íosa, a Íosa,
   Glóir agus moladh duit, a Íosa,
   Glóir agus moladh duit, a Shlánaitheoir,
   Glóir, moladh agus buíochas duit, Íosa, a Íosa.

Déanaimid 'Seo i gCuimhne ar Íosa

Eibhlín Nic Aoidh

Bernard Sexton

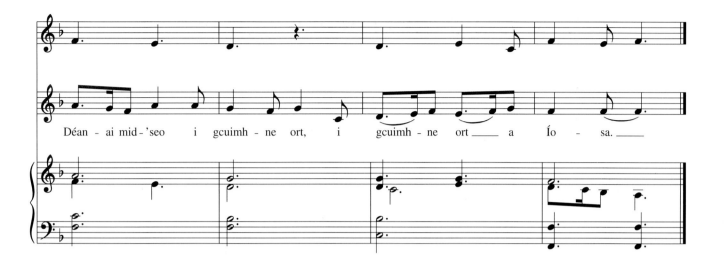

Déan - ai mid - 'seo i gcuimh - ne ort, i gcuimh - ne ort ___ a Ío - sa. ___

2. Molaimid Íosa le chéile
    Nuair a bhímid ag obair le chéile,
    Mise 'gus tusa – ár gcairde go léir,
    Ag caint is ag cabhrú, ag smaoineamh, ag plé.
    Déanaimid 'seo i gcuimhne ort, i gcuimhne ort a Íosa…

3. Molaimid Íosa le chéile
    Nuair a ithimid béile le chéile,
    Mise 'gus tusa – ár gcairde go léir,
    Ag roinnt is ag gáire, taobh le taobh.
    Déanaimid 'seo i gcuimhne ort, i gcuimhne ort a Íosa…

Do This in Memory of Jesus

Cyril Murphy

Do this in me-mory of Je - - sus.

Do this in me-mory of Je - - sus.

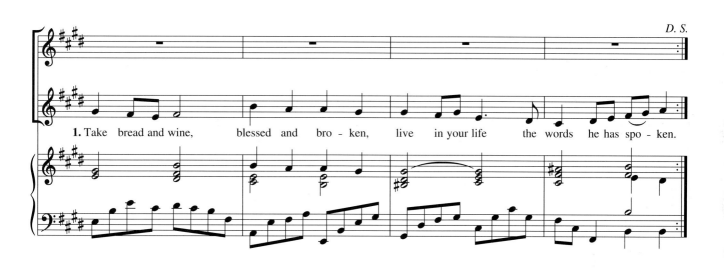

1. Take bread and wine, blessed and bro - ken, live in your life the words he has spo - ken.

2. Trust in his love, Walk in his ways. Share with the world his peace, his praise.

Eat This Bread

Jacques Berthier
(1923-1994)

Eat this bread, drink this cup, come to me and ne - ver be hun - gry.

Fine

Eat this bread, drink this cup, trust in me and you will not thirst.

D. C. al Fine

A - ny one who eats this bread will live for - e - ver.

Gather Round
Bailímis le Chéile

Fr Peter O'Reilly
Máire Nuinseann

Fr Peter O'Reilly

Voice: We ga-ther in bo-dy, we ga-ther in mind, __ in peace and in qui-et, to-ge-ther to find __ God's Ho-ly Spi-rit round and a-bout us, Through us, with us and in us.

Guth: Bail-í-mis le chéi-le le suaimh-neas ag-us grá. Bail-í-mis le chéi-le le suaimh-neas ag-us grá. Spior-ad Dé ion-ainn, thart tim-peall or-ainn, Trínn, linn ag-us ion-ainn.

Note: This piece works very effectively both in unison and as a round.

Go Now in Peace
Síocháin Libh

Gráinne Jordan
Fil Uí Dhubhghaill

Gráinne Jordan

1. Go now in peace to - ge - ther to-day. Je - sus is here in a ve - ry spe - cial way.

1. Im - igh a - nois i sío - cháin Dé, Beidh Ío - sa leat i rith an lae in - niu.

Tell all you meet that he is gen - tle and kind. Praise him and love him in bo - dy, soul and mind. Go in

In - is do chách go bhfuil sé cin - eál - ta cóir. Tabhair dó ___ mol - adh is on - óir is glóir. Sío - cháin

Chorus

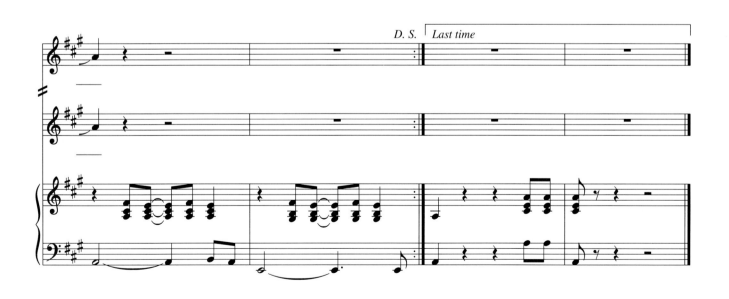

Go Now in Peace

2.   Bring all the love we've had here today.
Share it around, don't let it fade away.
Love one another as Jesus Christ loves you.
Praise him and love him in everything you do.

Síocháin Libh

2.   Beir leat an grá, a fuair tú anseo,
Roinn é go fial, ná lig dó dul amú.
Tabhair grá dá chéile, mar a ghráigh Íosa tú.
Mol é, is gráigh é le gach a ndéanann tú.

Happy in the Presence
Tagaimis le Chéile

Bernard Sexton

Happy in the pre-sence of the Lord, We come and sing our praise to Lord Je - sus.

Tag-ai-mis le chéi - le chuig an Tiar - na. Can - ai-mis is tug-ai-mis glóir dó.

Happy in the pre-sence of the Lord. We come and sing our praise to the Lord of all.

Tag-ai-mis le chéi - le chuig an Tiar Na. Can - ai-mis is tug-ai-mis gló - ir dó.

1. Come and share the bread of life, _ Bread that will feed _ us, help and pro-tect _ us.

1. Ith - im - is an t-ar - án beo, _ Ar - án na bea _ tha, inn - iu is go deo. _

Come and share the sto-ries of old, _ Sto-ries of Je - sus, his work and his world. _

Éis - ti - mis leis an dea - scéal faoi ob - air Ío - sa is _ a shaol. _

Coda

all. We come and sing _ our praise to the Lord _ of all.

dó.

Coda

25

Happy in the Presence

2.   Come and share the mem'ries we've had,
Happy days, sad days, days full of joy.
Come to tell the Lord that we love
We'll live the life he told us to live.

Tagaimis le Chéile

2.   Bímis ag cuimhneamh le chéile,
Brónach bhí muid trá, anois riméadach.
Tagaimis chuig a bhéile,
Tógaimis slí an ghrá go deo.

I Am the Bread

Clare Maloney

Mary Nugent

2. We your people gather round your table to be fed.
Thank you for your presence in the word,
in people, in priest, in bread.

I Remember
Is Maith is Cuimhin Liom

Geraldine Doggett
Eibhlín Nic Aoidh

Geraldine Doggett

I Remember

2. I remember, I remember
    All the stories people read
    About what Jesus did and said.
    These stories I bring today.
    Accept my gifts, O Lord I pray, Lord I pray.

3. I remember, I remember
    Jesus sharing one last time
    With his friends the bread and wine.
    This bread and wine I bring today.
    Accept my gifts, O Lord I pray, Lord I pray.

Is Maith is Cuimhin Liom

2. Is maith is cuimhin liom an scéal
    Faoi Íosa ar an saol fadó,
    Ag guí, ag caint, ár gcara beo.
    Na scéalta breátha i mo chroí,
    Tugaim duit, a Thiarna Dia,
    A Thiarna Dia.

3. Is maith is cuimhin liom an scéal,
    Bheannaigh Íosa arán is fíon,
    A chairde ag ithe lena thaobh,
    Na bronntanais arán is fíon,
    Tugaim duit, a Thiarna Dia,
    A Thiarna Dia.

I'm Sorry
Tá Brón Orm

Geraldine Doggett
Moya Ní Cheallaigh

Geraldine Doggett

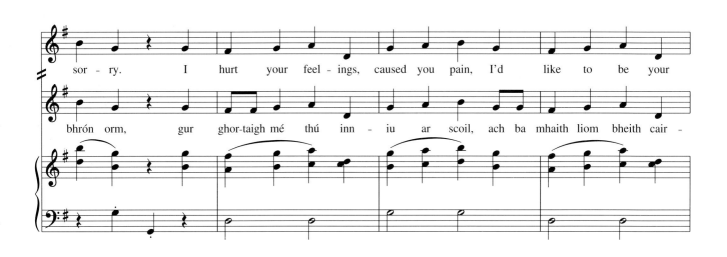

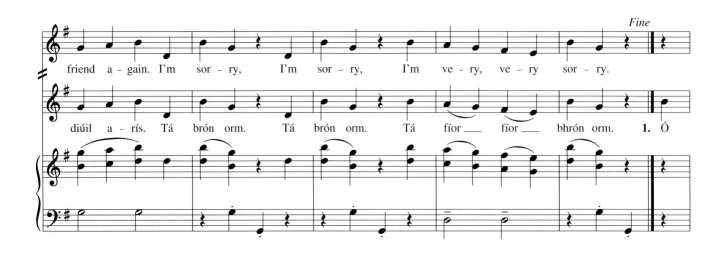

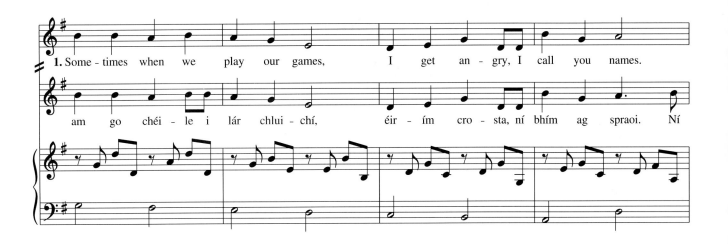

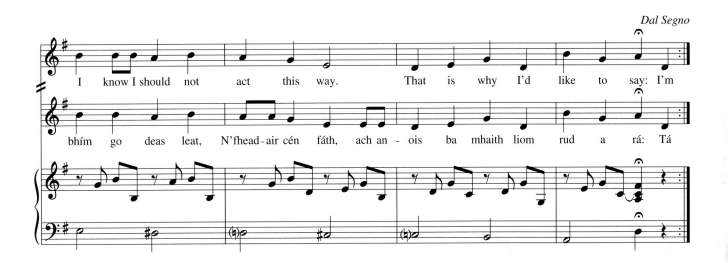

I'm Sorry

2. Sometimes I tell tales on you,
   I make up stories that are not true.
   I know I should not act this way,
   That is why I'd like to say…

3. Sometimes I won't let you play,
   I turn my back till you go away.
   I know I should not act this way,
   That is why I'd like to say…

Tá Brón Orm

2. Ó am go chéile insím scéalta
   Nach bhfuil fíor, níl ann ach bréaga.
   Ní bhím go deas leat,
   N'fheadair cén fáth,
   Ach anois ba mhaith liom rud a rá:

I'm Sorry, God

Mary Amond O'Brien

Lyrics:

Chorus
God wraps us in his love each day __ speaks gen-tly to us on our way. __ E-ven when we dis-o-bey, __ God's love is al-ways there. God loves us ev-'ry day.

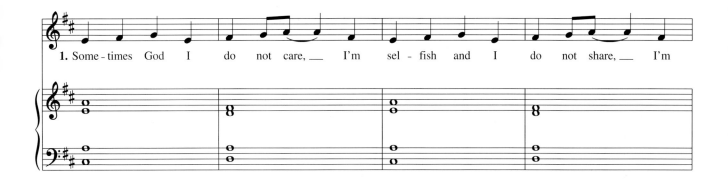

1. Some - times God I do not care, ___ I'm sel - fish and I do not share, ___ I'm

Dal Segno

sor - ry, God. Now I've come to know. ___ God

2.   Sometimes God I tell a lie
     Or hurt my friends and make them cry.
     I'm sorry, God,
     Now I've come to know…

3.   When I'm angry, God, I shout,
     I scream, I stamp and I give out.
     I'm sorry, God,
     Now I've come to know…

Ithigí an t-Arán Seo

Seán McCorraidh

Bernard Sexton

Ith - i - gí an t-ar - án __ seo, Ól - ai - gí as an gcai - lís __ seo.

Tag-a - gí chugam is ní bheidh or-aibh oc - ras, Cuir-i - gí bhur muin - ín ion-am, 's ní bheidh or - aibh __

tart. An té a ith - eann an t-ar - án seo, Mair - fidh sé go __ brách.

36

Maith Dom é, a Dhia

Eibhlín Nic Aoidh

Antaine Ó Faracháin

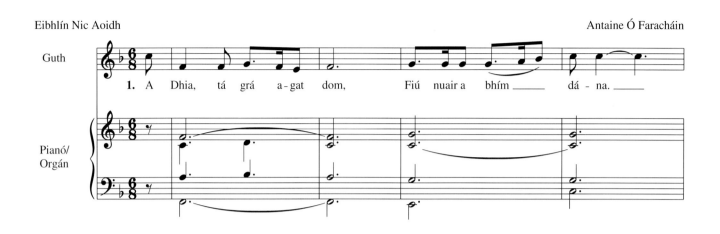

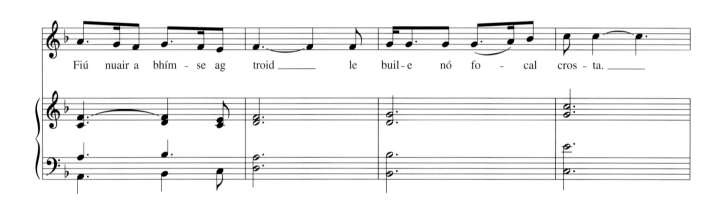

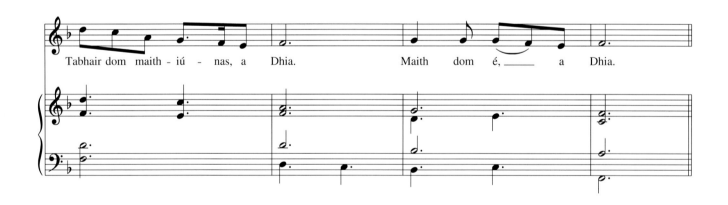

2.   A Dhia, tá grá agat dom
Fiú nuair a deirim 'Ní dhéanfaidh'.
Fiú nuair a insím bréag
'S nuair a ghortaím daoine eile.
Tabhair dom maithiúnas, a Dhia.
Maith dom é, a Dhia.

38

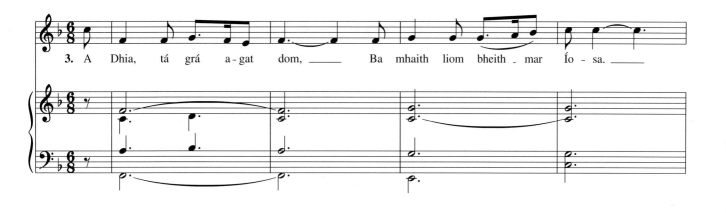

3. A Dhia, tá grá a - gat dom, _____ Ba mhaith liom bheith _ mar Ío - sa. _____

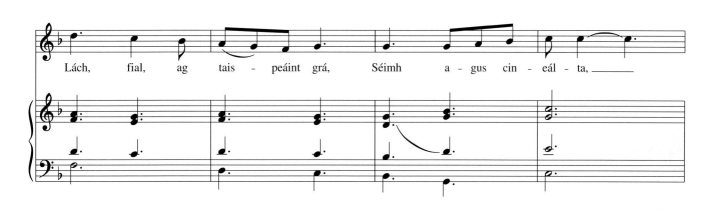

Lách, fial, ag tais - peáint grá, Séimh a - gus cin - eál - ta, _____

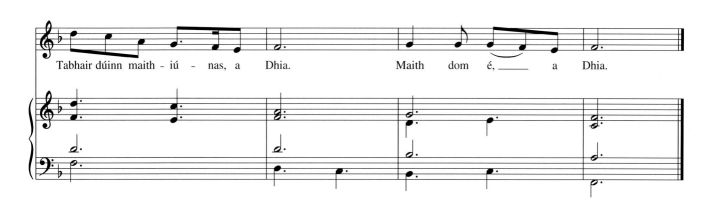

Tabhair dúinn maith - iú - nas, a Dhia. Maith dom é, _____ a Dhia.

Moladh le Dia

Máire Nuinseann

John McCann

Moladh le Dia! Mol - adh le Dia! Mol - adh go deo ___ le Di - a!

1. Réi - ti - mis an ál - tóir, Réi - ti - mis ál - tóir Dé, ___ le

héad - ach bán, geal ___ is glan, Mol - adh go deo le Di - a!

2.   Réitimis an áltóir,
     Réitimis áltóir Dé,
     Le coinnle lasta, geala, glé.
     Moladh go deo le Dia!

3.   Tugaimis an t-arán seo
     Le chéile chuig áltóir Dé.
     Déanfar arán na beatha de,
     Moladh go deo le Dia!

4.   Tugaimis an fíon seo
     Le chéile chuig áltóir Dé.
     Déanfar fuil Íosa de,
     Moladh go deo le Dia!

5.   Gabhaimis buíochas le chéile,
     Gabhaimis buíochas leat.
     Móraimid thú, adhraimid thú,
     Moladh go deo le Dia!

Nóta: Is féidir véarsa 1 agus 2 a fhágáil ar láir muna bhfuil an altóir réitithe ag an Ofráil.

My Shepherd is the Lord

Is é an Tiarna m'Aoire

Grace and Warren Brown
Eibhlín Nic Aoidh

Grace and Warren Brown

He shep-herds me.

Treor-aíonn sé mé.

My Shepherd Is The Lord

2. Sometimes when I'm afraid,
   Sad and all alone,
   You make my tears disappear
   With your touch of joy.
   You shepherd me.

3. You give me food to eat,
   Bless me every day.
   You give me rest as your guest
   Forever in your home.
   You shepherd me.

4. My shepherd is the Lord.
   He tends all my needs.
   By quiet streams he plants a dream
   Of peace and love for me.
   He shepherds me.

Is é an Tiarna m'Aoire

2. Cuid den am is mé tuirseach,
   Faoi ghruaim nó liom féin,
   Imíonn na deora uaimse
   Le fáilte mhór romhat féin,
   Treoraíonn tú mé.

3. Tugann tú dom bia,
   Beannaíonn tú mé gach lá,
   Iarrann tú orm suí go deo
   I do bhaile féin go sámh,
   Treoraíonn tú mé.

4. Is é an Tiarna m'aoire
   A thugann aire dom.
   Tá aisling lán de ghrá aige dom,
   Aisling lán de ghrá,
   Treoraíonn sé mé.

Remember Them
Cuimhnigh Orthu

Clare Maloney
Máire Nuinseann

Patricia Hegarty

Remember Them

2.   God keep them, God bless them,
      God shine your love on them
      Forever and forever, forever amen,
      Forever more, amen.

Cuimhnigh Orthu

2.   Tabhair aire dóibh is beannaigh iad,
      Na daoine a fuair bás.
      Suaimhneas agus síocháin leo,
      Is Dia go deo leo,
      Is Dia go deo leo.

Repeat verse 1   Véarsa 1 arís.

Stabat Mater

Clare Maloney

adapted from *Mainzish Gesangbuch,* 1661

At the cross her vi-gil keep-ing, Ma-ry stood in

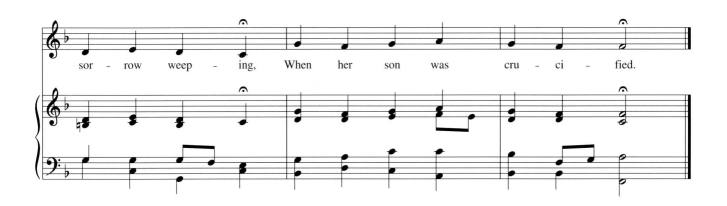

sor-row weep-ing, When her son was cru-ci-fied.

2. Hour of darkness descending.
   Mother, son; love unending,
   On the Hill of Calvary.

3. Mary, Mary crying.
   Slowly Jesus dying.
   Crucified, crucified.

4. Body, bowed and broken,
   Breath breathed, last word spoken.
   'Abba, Father! Amen.'

The Way to Be

Patricia Hegarty

Antaine Ó Faracháin

me. Be - ing kind and be - ing friend - ly, that's the way ___ to be.

2.   Most of the time, I'm fair, I'm true,
    My friends all trust me, I'm glad that they do.
    Some of the time, I tell a lie,
    Or leave someone out, and that makes them cry.
    Being unfair and being untruthful,
    That's not really me.
    Being fair and being truthful,
    That's the way to be!

This is the Day
Seo é an Lá

Mary Amond O'Brien
Fil Uí Dhubhghaill

Mary Amond O'Brien

50

made. _____

dúinn. _____

1. Let us re-joice and be glad, _____ This is the day the Lord has

1. Bíodh or-ainn glion-dar is áth - as, Seo é an lá 'thug an Tiar-na

made. Let us re-joice and be glad, This _____

dúinn. Bíodh or-ainn glion-dar croí. Seo _____

This is the Day

2. Play music to honour his name,
  This is the day the Lord has made.
  Sing psalms and songs of praise.
  This is the day.

Seo é an Lá

2. Seinn ceol ag moladh an Tiarna,
  Seo é an lá 'thug an Tiarna dúinn.
  Casaigí amhráin is ceol.
  Seo é an lá.

We Are the Greatest
Mo Chara Dílis

Clare Maloney
Antaine Ó Faracháin

Fran Hegarty

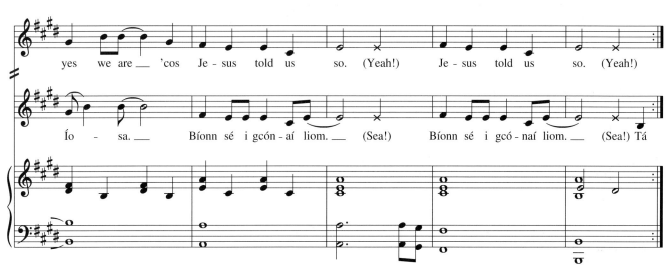

We Are the Greatest

2.   Just the way we children are
      Is just how we're happy to be,
      Full of surprises, full of love,
      Just how we're happy to be.
      And just in case there's any doubt
      We want you to know
      We are the greatest, yes we are
      'Cos Jesus told us so, Yeah!
      Jesus told us so, Yeah!

Mo Chara Dílis

2.   Tá aithne ag Íosa ormsa,
      Is cara mór liom é.
      Is breá leis a bheith ag cabhrú liom,
      Is cara mór leis mé.
      Mo chara dílis Íosa,
      Bíonn sé i gcónaí liom,
      Mo chara dílis Íosa,
      Bíonn sé i gcónaí liom, Sea!
      Bíonn sé i gcónaí liom, Sea!

We Come to You, Lord Jesus

Maura Kitching

1. We _

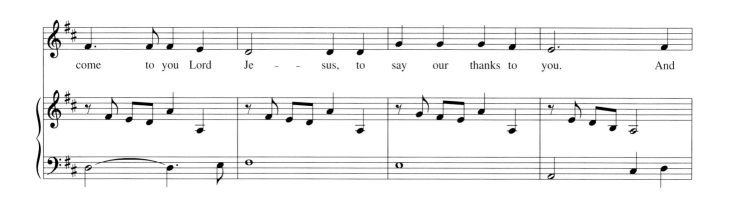

come   to you Lord   Je - - sus,   to   say   our   thanks to   you.   And

Chorus

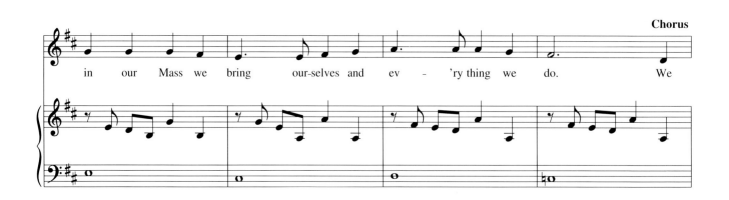

in   our   Mass   we   bring   our-selves   and   ev - 'ry thing   we   do.   We

58

love   you Lord Je - sus,   Stay   with us   we   pray.

Help   us to be more like you each day.

Last time

2.   We bring the bread, we bring the wine,
       We bring them now to you.
       We bring our work, we bring our play,
       And ev'ry thing we do.

3.   Your love for us, our love for you,
       We celebrate today.
       Oh fill our hearts with peace and joy.
       Be with us Lord we pray.

Alive-O Mass

Kyrie

Patricia Hegarty

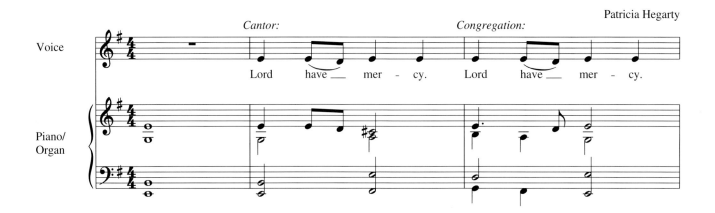

Gospel Acclamation

Patricia Hegarty

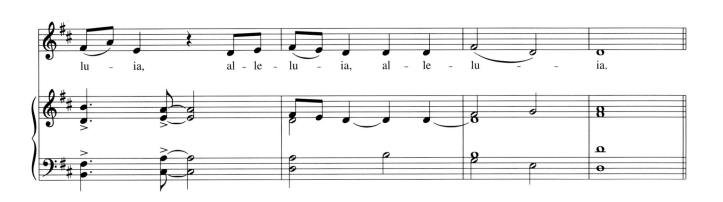

Sanctus

Patricia Hegarty

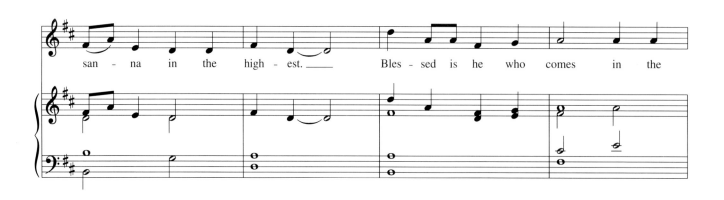

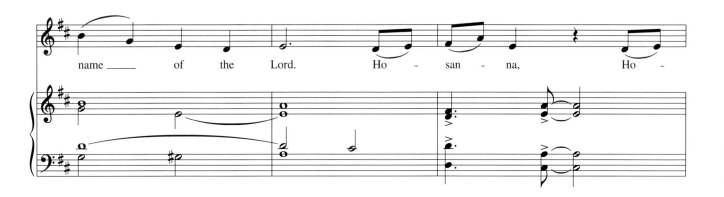

name _____ of the Lord. Ho - san - na, Ho -

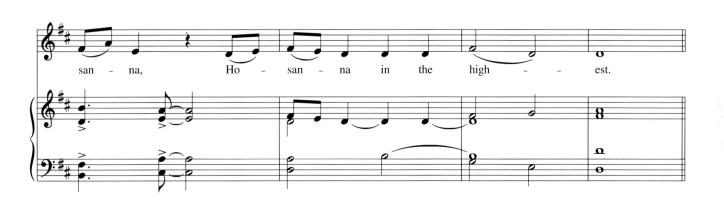

san - na, Ho - san - na in the high - - est.

Memorial Acclamation

Patricia Hegarty

Priest: Let us pro - claim the my - ste - ry of faith:

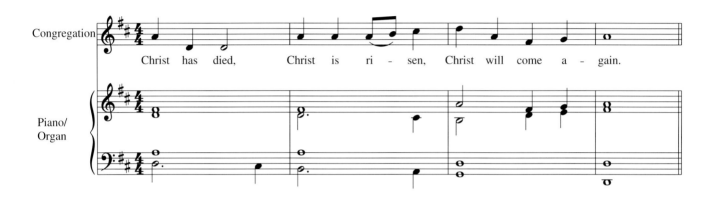

Congregation: Christ has died, Christ is ri - sen, Christ will come a - gain.

Doxology and Great Amen

Patricia Hegarty

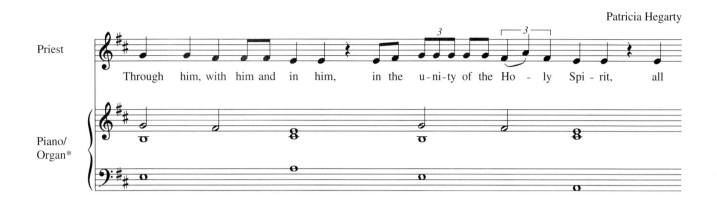

Through him, with him and in him, in the u-ni-ty of the Ho – ly Spi – rit, all

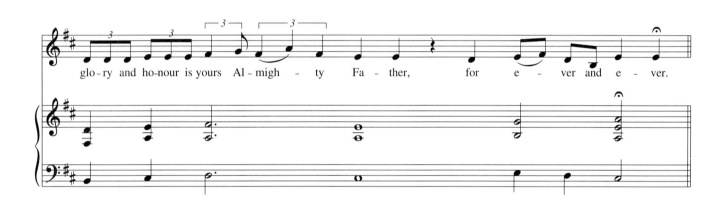

glo-ry and ho-nour is yours Al – migh – ty Fa – ther, for e – ver and e – ver.

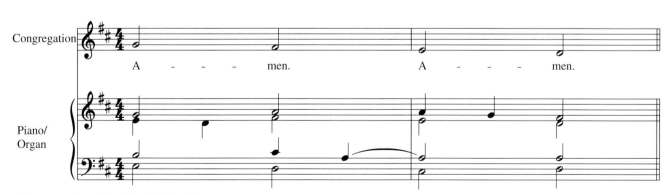

A – – men. A – – men.

*Accompaniment is optional in Doxology.

The Lord's Prayer

Patricia Hegarty

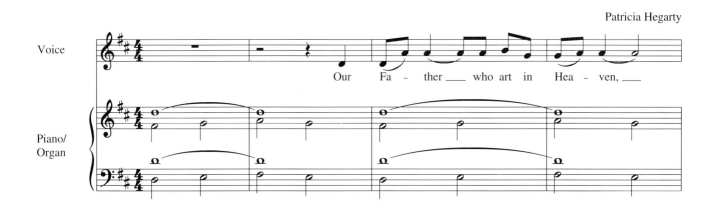

Our Fa - ther ___ who art in Hea - ven, ___

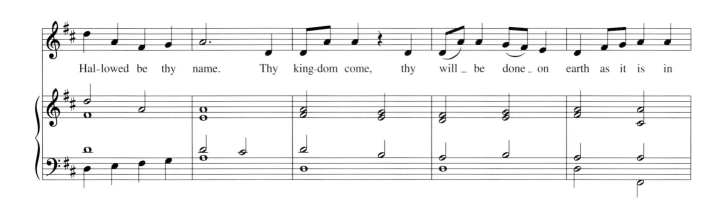

Hal - lowed be thy name. Thy king-dom come, thy will _ be done _ on earth as it is in

Hea - ven. ___ Give us this day our dai - ly bread. For - give ___ us our

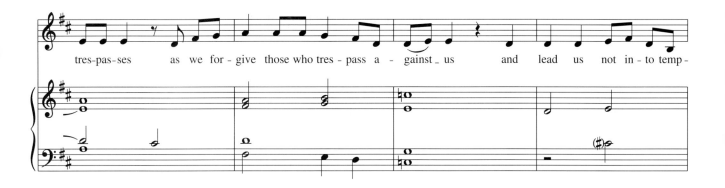

tres-pas-ses   as we for - give those who tres - pass a - gainst _ us   and lead us not in - to temp-

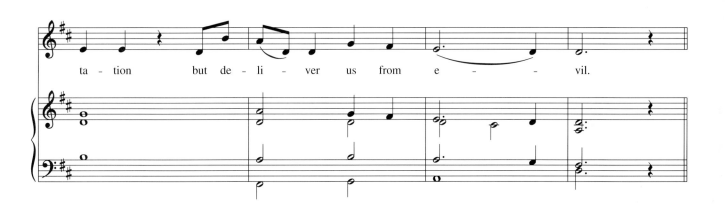

ta - tion   but de - li - ver us from e - - vil.

Agnus Dei

Patricia Hegarty

Aifreann

Kyrie

Ronan McDonagh

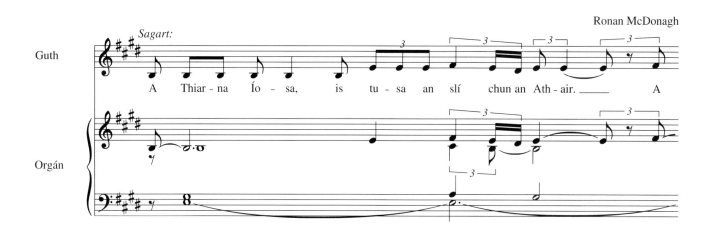

A Thiar - na Ío - sa, is tu - sa an slí chun an Ath - air. _____ A

Thiar - na, déan tró - cai - re. _____ A Thiar - na, déan tró - cai - re. _____ A

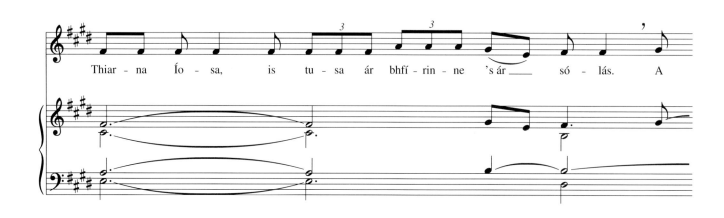

Thiar - na Ío - sa, is tu - sa ár bhfí - rin - ne 's ár _____ só - lás. A

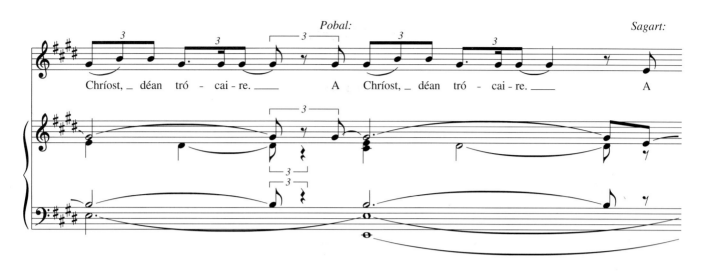

Chríost, __ déan tró - cai - re. __ A Chríost, __ déan tró - cai - re. __ A

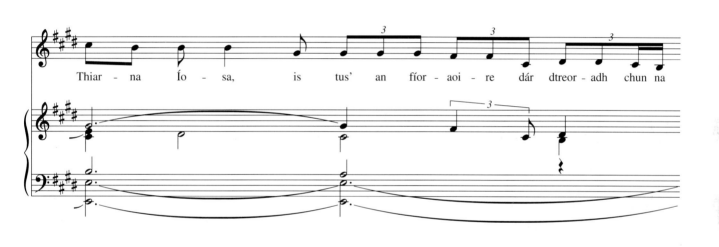

Thiar - na Ío - sa, is tus' an fíor - aoi - re dár dtreor - adh chun na

bhFlai - theas. A Thiar - na, déan tró - cai - re. __ A Thiar - na, déan tró - cai - re. __

Alleluia

Ronan McDonagh

Sanctus

Ronan McDonagh

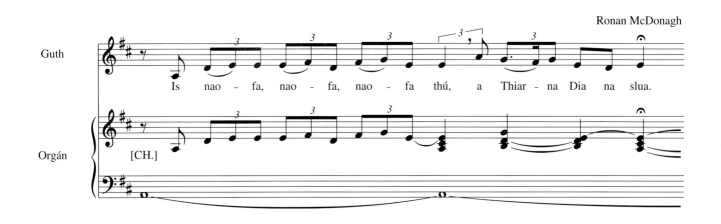

Is nao-fa, nao-fa, nao-fa thú, a Thiar-na Dia na slua.

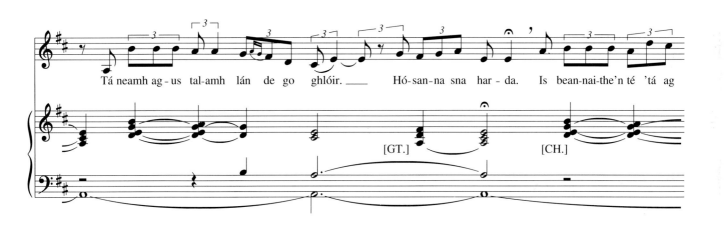

Tá neamh ag-us tal-amh lán de go ghlóir.____ Hó-san-na sna har-da. Is bean-nai-the'n té 'tá ag

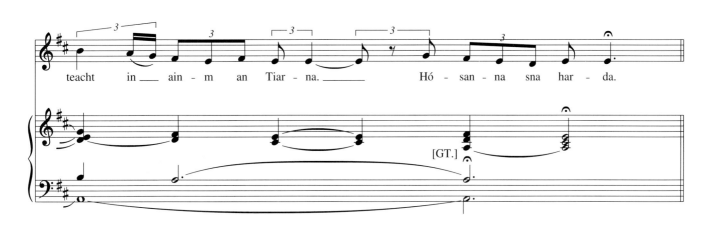

teacht in__ ain-m an Tiar-na._____ Hó-san-na sna har-da.

Fógra an Chreidimh

Ronan McDonagh

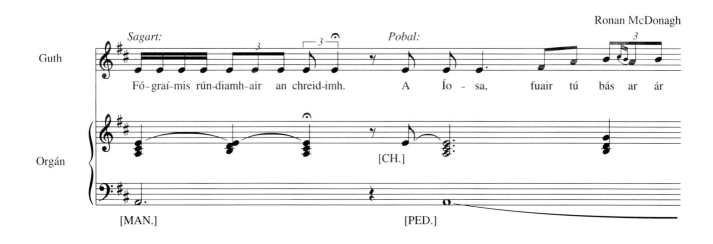

Fó-graí-mis rún-diamh-air an chreid-imh. A Ío - sa, fuair tú bás ar ár

son. D'éir - igh tú ó na mairbh. Tioc - faidh tú 'rís.

Amen

Ronan McDonagh

Guth / Orgán

Sagart:
Is tríd ag-us leis ag-us ann a thug-tar gach on-óir ag-us glóir duit-se, a Dhia an tAth-air ui-le-chumhach-tach, mar _ aon leis an Spior-ad Naomh, trí shaol na saol.

Pobal:
A - - - - - men.

An Phaidir

Ronan McDonagh

A Uain Dé

Ronan McDonagh

A Uain Dé, a thó - gas pea - caí an domhain, ___ déan tró - cai-re 'rainn. A Uain Dé, a thó - gas pea-caí an domhain, __ tabhair . dúinn sío-cháin.

Acknowledgements

Veritas Publications sincerely thanks the following authors, composers and owners or holders of copyright who have so kindly granted permission to use their material.

Ronan McDonagh for 'Aifreann'; Bernard Sexton, for 'Alleluia' (accompaniment); John McCann for 'Blessed Be God' and music of 'Moladh le Dia'; Cyril Murphy for 'Do This in Memory of Jesus' (accompaniment); Ateliers et Presses de Taizé, 71250 Taizé Community, France for 'Eat This Bread' © 1984; New Dawn Music, 5536 NE Hassalo, Portland, OR 97123, USA for 'My Shepherd is the Lord' by Grace and Warren Brown; Mary Amond O'Brien for 'This is the Day' and music of 'Seo é an Lá'.

All other songs are copyright of the Irish Episcopal Conference.
All other accompaniments written by Patricia Hegarty and Mary Nugent, copyright Veritas.